THE GO

Why Bad Things Happen

Andrew Wommack

Unless otherwise indicated, all Scripture quotations are taken from the *King James Version* of the Bible.

The author has emphasised some words in Scripture quotations in italicised type.

Why Bad Things Happen
ISBN: 978-1-907159-06-0
© 2010 by Andrew Wommack Ministries - Europe
PO Box 4392 Walsall, WS1 9AR, England
www.awme.net

Printed in the UK by Bell and Bain, Glasgow.

Contents

Foreword

In the aftermath of the 2001 terrorist attacks on America, the question "Why do bad things happen?" has been asked more than usual. All too often, that question doesn't find an answer, or the wrong answer is given.

Some Christian leaders proclaimed that the attacks were God's judgment upon America. Others didn't blame God directly, but said that He allowed it.

Either one of those answers sends a signal that God is the one behind the bad things that happen to us. Is that what the Word of God teaches? Are these the only two choices we have for why bad things happen?

In this issue of The Good Report, we will seek to answer these and other questions related to the origin of trouble. You will find an explanation of what the sovereignty of God truly is. We'll deal with the scripture that says "All things work together for good" and use a great testimony to illustrate that. We'll reveal the authority God has given to man and explain why God allows what man allows. And, of course, we'll talk about Job.

This has to be one of the most basic questions ever asked of God. How we answer this question determines how we view the very nature of God. If we see God as the one who unleashes all of life's miseries, then we will find it hard to come into a loving relationship with Him. God isn't mad; He's not even in a bad mood. God loves us and is not the author of our troubles.

– Andrew Wommack

Is God Sovereign?

Many people would never question the sovereignty of God. In fact, I'm sure many consider it near blasphemy that I would say, "Is God sovereign?" But this bears examining.

The word "sovereign" is not used in the *King James Version* of the Bible. It is used 303 times in the Old Testament of the *New International Version*, but it is always used in association with the word "LORD" and is the equivalent of the *KJV's* "LORD God." Not a single one of those times is the word "sovereign" used in the manner that it has come to be used by many religious leaders.

The dictionary defines "sovereign" as

1) Paramount; supreme.

2) Having supreme rank or power.

3) Independent: a sovereign state.

4) Excellent.

None of these definitions mean God controls everything. Religion has invented a new meaning for the word "sovereign," which basically means that God controls everything – nothing can happen but what He wills or allows. This is a doctrine of convenience and is not scriptural.

It is supposed that since God is paramount, or supreme, nothing can happen without His approval. That is not what the Scriptures teach. In 2 Peter 3:9, Peter said, *"The Lord is...not willing that any should perish, but that all should come to repentance."* This very clearly states that it is not the Lord's will for anyone to perish, but people are perishing. In fact, Jesus said, *"Enter ye in at the strait gate: for wide is the gate, and broad is the way, that leadeth to destruction, and many there be which go in thereat"* (Matt. 7:13). Relatively few people are saved compared to the number that are lost. God's will for people concerning salvation is not being accomplished.

This is because the Lord gave us the freedom to choose. He doesn't will anyone to hell. He paid for the sins of the whole world (1 John 2:2 and 1 Tim. 4:10), but we must choose to put our faith in Christ and receive His salvation. People are the ones choosing hell by not choosing Jesus as their Savior. It is the free will of man that damns them, not God.

Men literally have to climb over the roadblocks God puts in their way to continue on their course to hell. The cross of Christ and the drawing power of the Holy Spirit are obstacles that every sinner encounters. No one will ever stand before God and be able to fault Him for not giving them the opportunity to be saved. The Lord woos ever person to Himself, but we have to cooperate. Ultimately, the Lord simply enforces the consequences of people's own choices.

God has a perfect plan for every person's life (Jer. 29:11), but He doesn't make us walk that path. We are free moral agents with the ability to choose. He has told us what the right choices are (Deut. 30:19), but He doesn't make those choices for us. God gave us the power to control our destinies.

James 4:7 says, *"Submit yourselves therefore to God. Resist the devil, and he will flee from you."* This verse makes it very clear that some things are from God and some are from the devil. We must submit to the things that are of God and resist the things that are from the devil. The word "resist" means "to actively fight against." Saying "Whatever will be, will be" is not actively fighting against the devil.

If a person really believed that God is the One who put sickness on them because He is trying to work some good in their life, then they should not go to the doctor or take any medicine. That would be resisting God's plans. They should let the sickness run its course and thereby get the full benefit of God's correction. Of course, no one advocates that. That is absurd. It's even more absurd to believe that God is the one behind our tragedies.

Acts 10:38 says that Jesus healed all those who were oppressed OF THE DEVIL. It was not God who oppressed them with sickness; it was the devil. It's the same today. Sickness is from the devil, not God. We are to resist sickness and, by faith, submit ourselves to healing, which is from God through the atonement of Christ.

I know someone is thinking, *What about the Old Testament instances where God smote people with sickness and plagues?* There is a lot that I could say about that, but space doesn't allow. A simple answer to that question is that none of those instances were blessings; they were curses. God did use sickness in the Old Testament as punishment, but in the New Testament, Jesus bore our curse for us (Gal. 3:13). The

Lord would no more put sickness on a New Testament believer than He would make us commit sin. Both forgiveness of sin and healing are a part of Jesus' atonement.

Knowing that God is not the author of my problems has been one of the most important revelations the Lord ever gave me. If I thought it was God who killed my father when I was twelve; and some of my friends before I was twenty; if it was God who had people kidnap me, slander me, threaten to kill me, and turned loved ones against me; then I would have a hard time trusting a God like that.

On the contrary, it is very comforting to know that God only has good things in store for me. **Any problems in my life are from the devil, of my own making, or just the results of life on a fallen planet.** My heavenly Father has never done me any harm and never will. I KNOW that.

If hardship and problems make us better, then everyone who has had problems would be better for them. And those who had the most trouble would be the best. That simply is not so.

God is sovereign in the sense that He is paramount and supreme. There is no one higher in authority or power. But that does not mean He exercises his power in a way that He controls everything in our lives. God has given us the freedom to choose. He has a plan for us, and He seeks to reveal that plan to us and urge us in that direction. But we choose. He doesn't make our choices for us.

In many instances, it is our wrong choices that bring disaster upon us. In other cases, our problems are nothing but nature taking its course.

I believe this is the worst doctrine in the church today. I know that is a shocking statement which may offend people, but the way "sovereignty" is taught today is a real faith-killer. The belief that God controls everything is one of the devil's biggest inroads into our lives. If God controls everything, then our actions are irrelevant, and our efforts meaningless. Whatever will be, will be.

Believing that God wills everything to happen, good or bad, gives us some temporary relief from confusion and condemnation. In the long term, though, it slanders God, hinders our trust in Him, and leads to passivity.

Andrew's teaching "Sovereignty of God" (Item Code: L03C) explains this subject more fully.

3

God Allows What We Allow

This will come as a total shock to most people, but God doesn't directly control what happens on earth. He is the Creator of heaven and earth, and therefore, He has the ultimate authority over them. But, He has delegated the control of the earth to mankind.

In Genesis 1:26-28, God gave mankind dominion over this earth. This wasn't a conditional dominion that would be taken back if used incorrectly. No, there were no restrictions placed on how man could use his authority. The Lord never intended for us to use it as we have, but He has never broken His Word to us.

Psalm 89:34 says, *"My covenant will I not break, nor alter the thing that is gone out of my lips."* God's Word is binding, even on Himself. Hebrews 1:3 says that God upholds all things by the Word of His power. If He ever broke His Word, this world would self-destruct. Therefore, when mankind began to use his God-given authority to work evil, God could not just intervene and set things straight. He had given us the earth (Ps.115:16), and it was ours to do with as we pleased. He gave us His Word on it.

That's why Jesus had to become a man. Only mankind had authority on the earth. So, God became a man. God was no longer just a spirit (John 4:24); He had become flesh and blood also, and therefore had authority on the earth again (John 5:27). Jesus used this authority as a man to gain back what we lost. Before He headed back to His Father, Jesus said, *"All power is given unto me in heaven and in earth"* (Matt. 28:18). Then He shared that power and authority with all His saints.

The authority that mankind lost to the devil has been restored to man, but it is a shared authority with Jesus. That means it will never fall into the devil's hands again, because, regardless of our unfaithfulness, Jesus will never fail. That also means that the Lord has to have our cooperation to exercise His authority, because it's a shared authority. This is why bad things happen.

The Lord doesn't directly control the events on earth. He has a plan, but that plan has to have our cooperation to come to pass. Ephesians 3:20 says, *"Now unto him that is able to do exceeding abundantly above all that we ask or think, according to the power that worketh in us."* Notice that the Lord limited what He would do according to the power that works in us. If there isn't any power, then what He wants for us will not come to pass.

So, in a very real sense, He is not the One who allows evil on the earth – we are. God allows what we allow, because God has to work through us.

This is a very brief summary of a six-part album Andrew has entitled Spiritual Authority. Item Code: 1017C

All Things Work Together For Good

One of the most familiar and most misused scriptures in the Bible is Romans 8:28. This verse says, *"And we know that all things work together for good to them that love God, to them who are the called according to his purpose."*

First of all, notice what this verse does not say. It does not say that God causes all things. It is simply saying that God can work all things to our good, but even that is conditional.

This verse starts with the conjunction "and." That means this verse is dependent on the preceding verses. Verses 26 and 27 were talking about the Holy Spirit interceding through us. The Holy Spirit doesn't intercede for us, but through us. It's only when we are allowing that intercession that all things work together for our good.

Also, notice in verse 28 that this only happens for those who love God. This isn't a promise to unbelievers, or even to carnal Christians. This is for those who are truly in love with God. It goes on to say in verse 28 that this also only works for those who are called according to His purpose. What is the purpose of the Lord? First John 3:8 says, *"For this purpose the Son of God was manifested, that he might destroy the works of the devil."* In other words, only those who are resisting the devil and actively seeking to destroy the devil's works will have everything work together for their good.

Romans 8:28 does not mean that whatever happens to anyone comes from God and will work out for their good. That is not true, and every person knows that's not true. Romans 8:28 is a promise to believers who are allowing the Holy Spirit to work through them, who are in love with the Lord, and who are destroying Satan's works. Whatever happens to them will work together for their good.

The following is a modern-day example of how Romans 8:28 works:

The Storm Couldn't Blow Them Away

In 45 seconds, the life and ministry of Bob and Joy Nichols, and all of their church members, totally changed. The date was

March 28, 2000. The Nichols were in their office at Calvary Cathedral in Ft. Worth, Texas, when two tornadoes collided over their church building. The 100 people who were in the church building all miraculously escaped serious injury, but the church was a total loss. The 110,000 sq. ft. facility had to be completely torn down.

Within minutes, Bob was being interviewed by the news media. He said God hadn't done this to him, or to the church. However, he said God would take what the devil meant for evil and turn it around for good, that they would come out twice as good as before.

Instantly, God began to work miracles. Calvary's Christian school of 500 students was offered the facilities at a Church of Christ, just minutes from their old location. Churches and people from all over the city began to rally to their rescue. Newspaper reporters came to the following Sunday's services expecting a funeral, but instead they said, "They act like they just won the lottery." The church grew, and the finances stayed strong.

Calvary Cathedral met in a tent on the parking lot for months. Then the same Church of Christ that offered shelter to the school gave the use of their 2,000+ seat auditorium to Calvary Cathedral. They could buy the Church of Christ facility, remodel, build a new school for their students, and still have money left over. The location was better, and there were 27 acres instead of the 12+ acres at the old facility.

On top of all that, a major corporation bought the property that the old church building was located on for millions of dollars. So, in the end, things did work out together for good. They have twice as much land, twice as many buildings, and more than twice as much money on hand than before.

This tornado and its destruction was not an act of God, nor was it sent or allowed by God to try the people at Calvary Cathedral. Because the Nichols and the people of Calvary Cathedral loved God and resisted the devil's temptations to fear or become discouraged, God did work it together for good.

Andrew has an audio teaching (Item Code: L11C) which goes into more detail on Romans 8:28.

A Christian Response to the 2001 Terrorist Attack

I feel impressed of the Lord to respond to the terrorist attacks on the World Trade Centre in New York and the Pentagon in Washington, D.C. Everyone has been asking questions about why and how something like this could happen, and I feel the answers that most people are getting are woefully inadequate. God's Word has timeless answers that are right up-to-date for our current situation.

GOD DID NOT CAUSE, NOR DID HE ALLOW, THESE ATTACKS.

<u>Many Christian leaders have attributed these acts to the judgment of God upon America. That is absolutely not the case</u>. Jesus clearly stated that He did not come to destroy men's lives but to save them (Luke 9:56). This was said in response to His disciples wanting to call fire down from heaven on the Samaritans as judgment, just as Elijah had done in the Old Testament. Jesus wouldn't do it. In fact, He rebuked His disciples for desiring to do so, showing that God was dealing with the earth differently after the advent of Jesus.

There is a future time, described in the book of Revelation, when God's judgment will rain down upon the unbelievers, but today we are living in an age of grace when God is not imputing man's sins unto him (2 Cor. 5:19). There were, no doubt, godly men and women who lost their lives in these terrorist attacks. God certainly wasn't judging them.

If this had been God's judgment, it would have been much more severe. In the Old Testament, when God's judgment was being released, a death angel went through the land of Egypt and killed all the first born (Ex. 12:29-30). Another angel killed 185,000 Assyrians in one night (2 Kings 19:35).

The Lord wouldn't have had to use suicide bombers to accomplish His judgment. These men were deceived into thinking they would be granted a special place in heaven with a harem of women if they would kill innocent men, women, and children. That doesn't sound like God. That's not God's "method of operation." In the Old Testament, God had the earth open up and swallow people and then close over them again (Num. 16:28-33). Sodom and Gomorrah was completely destroyed by fire from heaven, and Noah's flood destroyed all but eight people on the earth (Gen. 7).

Why would the Lord only judge America and not other nations? Or, why would New York and the Pentagon be the targets instead of the centers of homosexuality or the movie industry, which has defied God? Why didn't God judge non-Christian nations that make America look moral by comparison?

No, this was not God's judgment. America is worthy of judgment, but God is extending grace to America, as well as to all the other nations of the world during this church age. There will come a time when God's judgment is released on the whole world, and no one will have to be told it's God doing the judging. The people will cry out for the rocks to fall upon them and hide them from the wrath of God (Rev. 6:12-17). But that time hasn't come yet.

This is not to say that there are no consequences for our national sins. The Scripture says, *"Righteousness exalteth a nation: but sin is a reproach to any people"* (Prov. 14:34). Sin allows the devil access to us (Rom. 6:16). Jesus said the devil comes only *"to steal, and to kill, and to destroy: I [Jesus] am come that they might have life, and that they might have it more abundantly"* (John 10:10, brackets mine). Satan, not God, inspired and carried out these attacks through demon-possessed people.

Some wouldn't go so far as to say that God commissioned these attacks, but they believe that nothing happens but what God allows. It's like saying that not all bad things originate from God's desk, but they all have to pass through there and get His stamp of approval. That's not the way God's kingdom works. There are lots of things that happen that are not in God's deliberate or permissive will.

I know some people just choked on that last statement. They think that is a direct attack on the sovereignty of God. God is so sovereign that He has limited Himself in the affairs of man. Indeed, Psalm 78:41 says that people in unbelief limited the Holy One of Israel.

Therefore, God didn't do this, nor did He allow it. It was free moral agents that rebelled at all of God's conviction who perpetrated this cowardly act. Any portrayal of God as the source of this tragedy misrepresents His nature and character to the lost. <u>There is no doubt that many people will be turned away from God because of ministers who attribute terrorist acts to God</u>.

Another point that I think is very important to correct is the error that this happened because the body of Christ hasn't done enough spiritual warfare. I was with a group of ministers when we got the news of the bombings, and this was the first reaction from some of them. They believed spiritual warfare could have prevented these attacks and that more spiritual warfare is the thing to stop this in the future. I think that is absolutely wrong.

First of all, if there has been an excess of anything in the body of Christ over the last ten years, it is in the area of spiritual warfare. There have been entire conferences dedicated to the subject, and millions of believers have gotten involved. I believe it is safe to say that there have been more people doing spiritual warfare in the last decade than in all of church history. Yet, it will not stop ungodly people from being ungodly!

If you follow that logic, then it was the lack of spiritual warfare that caused the bombing of Pearl Harbor and started America's involvement in World War II. Are you willing to make that indictment? Most would have to say that America was much more godly then than now.

There are scriptural examples of godly kings who had nations attack them in war, and it wasn't because of some lack on their part (2 Chr. 20). Bad things happen to good people and good nations. Every problem cannot be prayed away. The Lord doesn't promise that we won't have trouble. In fact, He promised us that we would have tribulation, but He told us to be of good cheer even then because He has overcome the world (John 16:33). We are guaranteed to come out winners.

When nations take deliberate steps away from God, as America has, they walk out from God's umbrella of protection. God doesn't punish them directly, but there will be punishment. Satan will exact his own wrath on those who yield to him. As Jonah said, *"They that observe lying vanities forsake their own mercy"* (Jon. 2:8). He ought to know. God is a good God, but the devil is a bad devil.

If we, as Americans, would turn to the Lord with all our hearts, then we would see more supernatural protection and intervention on our behalf. No nation has ever, or will ever, trust God perfectly. Therefore, there will always be the potential for these types of acts.

Also, if the body of Christ had been to the Islamic world, then there would have been the potential that these terrorists would have been converted, as Saul was, and these acts would not have happened. However, men have the free will to choose, and there's no guarantee that everyone will receive the Gospel. There will always be some who hate God and everything that reflects godly values, and who are willing to fight against the things of God.

As individuals, we can appropriate God's supernatural protection on a personal level, but we can't throw that net across the entire nation when vast amounts of Americans are in total rebellion to the Lord. As long as we live in a world where people yield to Satan's deception, then there will be wars.

What should be a Christian response to what the terrorists have done? Should we forgive them and turn the other cheek? Isn't that what Jesus taught?

Look at what Jesus told Pilate just before His crucifixion. Jesus said, *"My kingdom is not of this world: if my kingdom were of this world, then would my servants fight, that I should not be delivered to the Jews"* (John 18:36). Jesus didn't resist the Roman or Jewish authority, because He wasn't establishing a physical kingdom. His kingdom was in the hearts of men (Luke 17:20-21). His spiritual kingdom could not have been established by physical means, so He submitted to their power.

A time is coming when the Lord will establish a physical kingdom here on the earth, and then blood will flow up to the horses' bridles (Rev. 14:20). This establishes a principle that if you are fighting a physical foe, you use physical weapons. If you are fighting a spiritual foe, you use spiritual weapons.

I've been spit upon, cussed at, threatened, kidnapped, slandered, hated, and much more because of my teaching of the Gospel. In all these things, I've not fought back or resisted, because all these things happened for the Gospel's sake. I took it as persecution. But, if someone was to try and rob me, just to get my $20, I would fight back. If someone threatened my wife with bodily harm, I would fight to the death to protect her. Anyone who would not do the same for their wife is "whack."

Sure, the Lord said to turn the other cheek and resist not evil (Matt. 5:39), but this same Jesus made a whip and drove the money changers from the temple. He didn't do it politely either. He *drove* the money changers from the temple. He didn't say, "I'm sorry. I hope you aren't offended. I have to do this." No! He was angry and He violently fought against them – not because of their personal attacks on Him but in defence of His Father.

On an individual level, we need to forgive others and not seek vengeance, but on a national level, government has the God-given responsibility to defend its citizens. The Scripture says, *"He beareth not the sword in vain: for he* [government] *is the minister of God, a revenger to execute wrath upon him that doeth evil"* (Rom. 13:4, brackets mine).

These terrorist attacks were pure evil, and the American government has a God-given responsibility to do whatever it takes to punish the perpetrators. No one wants innocent people to die, and I don't believe the current administration is seeking to retaliate blindly. This evil is like a cancer that has to be cut out and destroyed, even if it inflicts minimal damage to innocent people.

Some people have come to the conclusion that America was morally wrong to drop the two atomic bombs on Japan. They cite pictures of women and children who were killed or badly hurt in those bombings and say this couldn't be right. But they forgot the broader picture.

America and Japan were at war. The Japanese had exhibited unbelievable brutality in their actions during the war, especially toward the Chinese. The emperor, who was believed to be a god, had already given the command to all Japanese to fight the Americans to the last woman and child. He had armed the women and children and taught them to fight, and there is no reason to believe they wouldn't have obeyed. If that had happened, there would not only have been hundreds of thousands of American lives lost, but multiplied millions of Japanese would have died too.

When all of this is considered, it was still a terrible thing that happened in Hiroshima and Nagasaki, but it was much more merciful than the alternative. Millions of Japanese lives were actually saved through these bombings.

Terrorists have waged war on America and on all freedom-loving people who don't subscribe to their fanatical views. They must be sought out and destroyed with as much precision as possible. Any groups or nations who support them should distance themselves from these terrorists or suffer the consequences. That is a godly response.

The day after the September 11, 2001 attacks, Andrew made four thirty-minute television shows to deal with this subject. Andrew later made a one-hour audio message covering the same material, and all this was immediately loaded onto our website and later broadcast on television. This teaching is available to you, or you can listen to it or download it from our website. Remember that the four television broadcasts which deal with this same issue are also on our website www.awme.net. If you would like that audio teaching free, you can call all our Helpline on +44 (0) 1922 473 300.

What About Job?

The book of Job is a very unique book of the Bible. Since there is no mention of the Law of God, or reference to the Jews in this book, it has been supposed that Job lived before the time of Abraham. This would make the book of Job the oldest book in the Bible. Also, the mention of Satan coming before God and the discussion between God and Satan about Job is unparalled in all of Scripture.

Those who promote that God is the author of all our problems lean heavily on the book of Job to justify their position. They say that God pointed Job out to Satan and instigated all the tragedy that came to Job. This comes primarily from Job 1:8 where God said to Satan, *"Hast thou considered my servant Job, that there is none like him in the earth, a perfect and an upright man, one that feareth God, and escheweth evil?"*

However, this verse doesn't say that the Lord "put" Satan on Job. The Lord simply knew that Satan was out to get Job, and He brought it out into the open. The Hebrew text actually says, "Have you set your heart on my servant Job?" There isn't anything in this verse to imply that God initiated this whole affair.

It is very clear that Satan was the instigator of all of Job's problems. The Lord had actually built a hedge of protection around Job (Job 1:10). Satan tried to get God to afflict Job (Job 1:11), but the Lord wouldn't do it. He did say that all Job possessed was in Satan's hands, but that was already true. In a sense, God's hedge of protection about Job wasn't just. Jesus hadn't died to reconcile man to God. The Old Testament covenants between God and the Jews weren't even in place. Therefore, Job was vulnerable to the devil.

Instead of God being the One who was afflicting Job, He was the One who was protecting him. Satan insisted that he had a right to afflict Job, which he did. Man had sold himself the devil, and his redemption hadn't taken place yet. Therefore, the Lord pulled the hedge back.

There are many theological issues in the book of Job, which we don't have the space to discuss here. The way God has been accused as the afflictor of Job is untrue. The Lord's pleasure was to bless Job, before and after Satan's attacks. In chapter 42 of Job, God blessed Job and gave him twice as much as he had before. Anyone who claims to be like Job has to come through their problems with twice as much as before.

Without going into detail, it will suffice to say that Job didn't have the covenants and redemption that we have as New Testament believers. Job didn't have the promise of James 1:13, which says *"Let no man say when he is tempted, I am tempted of God: for God cannot be tempted with evil, neither tempteth he any man."*

As New Testament believers, we have better covenants and promises than the Old Testament saints. God is for us and not against us. He doesn't use trials and temptations to make us perfect. Second Timothy 3:16-17 says, *"All scripture is given by inspiration of God, and is profitable for doctrine, for reproof, for correction, for instruction in righteousness: That the man of God may be perfect, thoroughly furnished unto all good works."* God uses His Word, not problems, for reproof and correction. That method will make us perfect and complete. We don't need plan B, or plan C. God's Word is enough.

That's not to say we can't learn from hardship. We certainly do. But that's not God's method. We all fail to learn from the Word, so we have to learn by hard knocks. But there is a better way. We need to understand that God isn't the author of our problems so that we can resist them. Passiveness toward our problems gives Satan an opportunity against us.

Andrew has an audio teaching on the book of Job with some unusual insights into what happened with Job. Item Code: L07-C1/2

God Is Love

First John 4:8 says, "*God is love.*" God doesn't just have some love; He is love. He is His nature and essence.

Crediting God with all the hurt and tragedy of this life destroys His image of love. If God was a man who killed women and children, and even His own children in the 2001 terrorist attacks, He would be arrested and punished. Contrary to what many religious leaders are saying, God is not the author of our problems.

There are instances of God's judgment in the Old Testament, and there are prophecies of God's coming judgment in the New Testament. In this current church age, however, God is reconciling man unto Himself, not holding their sins against them. That's the message He has given us to proclaim (2 Cor. 5:19).

Seeing God as a loving God who is working for us instead of against us is the foundation of our faith. Faith works by love (Gal. 5:6), and coming to a new understanding of God's faithful love will make our faith abound.

If you haven't given your heart to God because of the way He's often been misrepresented, then do it now. God loves you more than you could possibly imagine. He is not against you. He is for you. Please call our Helpline on +44(0) 1922 473 300 for our free teaching entitled "What Is a Christian?" or if you are already born again, take comfort in the fact that God is not the source of your troubles. Become a part of the solution by resisting evil and sharing your faith with others. We pray that the ministry in this issue of *The Good Report* will strengthen your faith in the goodness of God.

Scriptures from this booklet

Is God Sovereign?

2 Peter 3:9

The Lord is...not willing that any should perish, but that all should come to repentances.

Matt. 7:13

Enter ye in at the strait gate: for wide is the gate, and broad is the way, that leadeth to destruction, and many there be which go in thereat.

1 John 2:2

And he is the propitiation for our sins: and not for ours only, but also for the sins of the whole world.

1 Tim. 4:10

For therefore we both labour and suffer reproach, because we trust in the living God, who is the Saviour of all men, specially of those that believe.

Jer. 29:11

For I know the thoughts that I think toward you, saith the LORD, thoughts of peace, and not of evil, to give you an expected end.

Deut. 30:19

I call heaven and earth to record this day against you, that I have set before you life and death, blessing and cursing: therefore choose life, that both thou and thy seed may live:

James 4:7

Submit yourselves therefore to God. Resist the devil, and he will flee from you.

Acts 10:38

How God anointed Jesus of Nazareth with the Holy Ghost and with power: who went about doing good, and healing all that were oppressed of the devil; for God was with him.

Gal 3:13

Christ hath redeemed us from the curse of the law, being made a curse for us: for it is written, Cursed is every one that hangeth on a tree:

God Allows What We Allow

Gen 1:26-28

And God said, Let us make man in our image, after our likeness: and let them have dominion over the fish of the sea, and over the fowl of the air, and over the cattle, and over all the earth, and over every creeping thing that creepeth upon the earth.

So God created man in his own image, in the image of God created he him; male and female created he them. And God blessed them, and God said unto them, Be fruitful, and multiply, and replenish the earth, and subdue it: and have dominion over the fish of the sea, and over the fowl of the air, and over every living thing that moveth upon the earth.

Psalm 89:34

My covenant will I not break, nor alter the thing that is gone out of my lips.

Heb 1:3

Who being the brightness of his glory, and the express image of his person, and upholding all things by the word of his power, when he had by himself purged our sins, sat down on the right hand of the Majesty on high:

Ps 115:16

The heaven, even the heavens, are the LORD's: but the earth hath he given to the children of men.

John 4:24

God is a Spirit: and they that worship him must worship him in spirit and in truth.

John 5:27

And hath given him authority to execute judgment also, because he is the Son of man.

Matt 28:18

And Jesus came and spake unto them, saying, All power is given unto me in heaven and in earth.

Eph 3:20

Now unto him that is able to do exceeding abundantly above all that we ask or think, according to the power that worketh in us,

All Things Work Together For Good

Rom 8:26-28

Likewise the Spirit also helpeth our infirmities: for we know not what we should pray for as we ought: but the Spirit itself maketh intercession for us with groanings which cannot be uttered. And he that searcheth the hearts knoweth what is the mind of the Spirit, because he maketh intercession for the saints according to the will of God. And we know that all things work together for good to them that love God, to them who are the called according to his purpose.

1 John 3:8

He that committeth sin is of the devil; for the devil sinneth from the beginning. For this purpose the Son of God was manifested, that he might destroy the works of the devil.

A Christian Response to the 2001 Terrorist Attacks

Luke 9:56

For the Son of man is not come to destroy men's lives, but to save them. And they went to another village.

2 Cor 5:19

To wit, that God was in Christ, reconciling the world unto himself, not imputing their trespasses unto them; and hath committed unto us the word of reconciliation.

Ex 12:29-30

And it came to pass, that at midnight the LORD smote all the firstborn in the land of Egypt, from the firstborn of Pharaoh that sat on his throne unto the firstborn of the captive that was in the dungeon; and all the firstborn of cattle. And Pharaoh rose up in the night, he, and all his servants, and all the Egyptians; and there was a great cry in Egypt; for there was not a house where there was not one dead.

2 Kings 19:35

And it came to pass that night, that the angel of the LORD went out, and smote in the camp of the Assyrians an hundred fourscore and five thousand: and when they arose early in the morning, behold, they were all dead corpses.

Num 16:28-33

And Moses said, Hereby ye shall know that the LORD hath sent me to do all these works; for I have not done them of mine own mind. If these men die the common death of all men, or if they be visited after the visitation of all men; then the LORD hath not sent me. But if the LORD make a new thing, and the earth open her mouth, and swallow them up, with all that appertain unto them, and they go down quick into the pit; then ye shall understand that these men have provoked the LORD. And it came to pass, as he had made an end of speaking all these words, that the ground clave asunder that was under them: And the earth opened her mouth, and swallowed them up, and their houses, and all the men that appertained unto Korah, and all their goods. They, and all that appertained to them, went down alive into the pit, and the earth closed upon them: and they perished from among the congregation.

Gen 7

And the LORD said unto Noah, Come thou and all thy house into the ark; for thee have I seen righteous before me in this generation. Of every clean beast thou shalt take to thee by sevens, the male and his female: and of beasts that are not clean by two, the male and his female. Of fowls also of the air by sevens, the male and the female; to keep seed alive upon the face of all the earth. For yet seven days, and I will cause it to rain upon the earth forty days and forty nights; and every living substance that I have made will I destroy from off the face of the earth.

And Noah did according unto all that the LORD commanded him. And Noah was six hundred years old when the flood of waters was upon the earth. And Noah went in, and his sons, and his wife, and his sons' wives with him, into the ark, because of the waters of the flood.

Of clean beasts, and of beasts that are not clean, and of fowls, and of every thing that creepeth upon the earth, There went in two and two unto Noah into the ark, the male and the female, as God had commanded Noah. And it came to pass after seven days, that the waters of the flood were upon the earth.

In the six hundredth year of Noah's life, in the second month, the seventeenth day of the month, the same day were all the fountains of the great deep broken up, and the windows of heaven were opened. And the rain was upon the earth forty days and forty nights.

In the self same day entered Noah, and Shem, and Ham, and Japheth, the sons of Noah, and Noah's wife, and the three wives of his sons with them, into the ark; They, and every beast after his kind, and all the cattle after their kind, and every creeping thing that creepeth upon the earth after his kind, and every fowl after his kind, every bird of every sort. And they went in unto Noah into the ark, two and two of all flesh, wherein is the breath of life. And they that went in, went in male and female of all flesh, as God had commanded him: and the LORD shut him in.

And the flood was forty days upon the earth; and the waters increased, and bare up the ark, and it was lift up above the earth. And the waters prevailed, and were increased greatly upon the earth; and the ark went upon the face of the waters. And the waters prevailed exceedingly upon the earth; and all the high hills, that were under the whole heaven, were covered. Fifteen cubits upward did the waters prevail; and the mountains were covered. And all flesh died that moved upon the earth, both of fowl, and of cattle, and of beast, and of every creeping thing that creepeth upon the earth, and every man:

All in whose nostrils was the breath of life, of all that was in the dry land, died. And every living substance was destroyed which was upon the face of the ground, both man, and cattle, and the creeping things, and the fowl of the heaven; and they were destroyed from the earth: and Noah only remained alive, and they that were with him in the ark. And the waters prevailed upon the earth an hundred and fifty days.

Rev 6:12-17

And I beheld when he had opened the sixth seal, and, lo, there was a great earthquake; and the sun became black as sackcloth of hair, and the moon became as blood; And the stars of heaven fell unto the earth, even as a fig tree casteth her untimely figs, when she is shaken of a mighty wind. And the heaven departed as a scroll when it is rolled together; and every mountain and island were moved out of their places. And the kings of the earth, and the great men, and the rich men, and the chief captains, and the mighty men, and every bondman, and every free man, hid themselves in the dens and in the rocks of the mountains; And said to the mountains and rocks, Fall on us, and hide us from the face of him that sitteth on the throne, and from the wrath of the Lamb:

For the great day of his wrath is come; and who shall be able to stand?

Prov 14:34

Righteousness exalteth a nation: but sin is a reproach to any people.

Rom 6:16

Know ye not, that to whom ye yield yourselves servants to obey, his servants ye are to whom ye obey; whether of sin unto death, or of obedience unto righteousness?

John 10:10

The thief cometh not, but for to steal, and to kill, and to destroy: I am come that they might have life, and that they might have it more abundantly.

Ps 78:41

Yea, they turned back and tempted God, and limited the Holy One of Israel.

2 Chr 20

It came to pass after this also, that the children of Moab, and the children of Ammon, and with them other beside the Ammonites, came against Jehoshaphat to battle. Then there came some that told Jehoshaphat, saying, There cometh a great multitude against thee from beyond the sea on this side Syria; and, behold, they be in Hazazontamar, which is Engedi. And Jehoshaphat feared, and set himself to seek the LORD, and proclaimed a fast throughout all Judah. And Judah gathered themselves together, to ask help of the LORD: even out of all the cities of Judah they came to seek the LORD. And Jehoshaphat stood in the congregation of Judah and Jerusalem, in the house of the LORD, before the new court, And said, O LORD God of our fathers, art not thou God in heaven? and rulest not thou over all the kingdoms of the heathen? and in thine hand is there not power and might, so that none is able to withstand thee?

Art not thou our God, who didst drive out the inhabitants of this land before thy people Israel, and gavest it to the seed of Abraham thy friend for ever? And they dwelt therein, and have built thee a sanctuary therein for thy name, saying,

If, when evil cometh upon us, as the sword, judgment, or pestilence, or famine, we stand before this house, and in thy presence, (for thy name is in this house,) and cry unto thee in our affliction, then thou wilt hear and help. And now, behold, the children of Ammon and Moab and mount Seir, whom thou wouldest not let Israel invade, when they came out of the land of Egypt, but they turned from them, and destroyed them not; Behold, I say, how they reward us, to come to cast us out of thy possession, which thou hast given us to inherit. O our God, wilt thou not judge them? for we have no might against this great company that cometh against us; neither know we what to do: but our eyes are upon thee.

And all Judah stood before the LORD, with their little ones, their wives, and their children.

Then upon Jahaziel the son of Zechariah, the son of Benaiah, the son of Jeiel, the son of Mattaniah, a Levite of the sons of Asaph, came the Spirit of the LORD in the midst of the congregation;

And he said, Hearken ye, all Judah, and ye inhabitants of Jerusalem, and thou king Jehoshaphat, Thus saith the LORD unto you, Be not afraid nor dismayed by reason of this great multitude; for the battle is not yours, but God's. To morrow go ye down against them: behold, they come up by the cliff of Ziz; and ye shall find them at the end of the brook, before the wilderness of Jeruel. Ye shall not need to fight in this battle: set yourselves, stand ye still, and see the salvation of the LORD with you, O Judah and Jerusalem: fear not, nor be dismayed; to morrow go out against them: for the LORD will be with you.

And Jehoshaphat bowed his head with his face to the ground: and all Judah and the inhabitants of Jerusalem fell before the LORD, worshipping the LORD. And the Levites, of the children of the Kohathites, and of the children of the Korhites, stood up to praise the LORD God of Israel with a loud voice on high.

And they rose early in the morning, and went forth into the wilderness of Tekoa: and as they went forth, Jehoshaphat stood and said, Hear me, O Judah, and ye inhabitants of Jerusalem; Believe in the LORD your God, so shall ye be established; believe his prophets, so shall ye prosper. And when he had consulted with the people, he appointed singers unto the LORD, and that should praise the beauty of holiness, as they went out before the army, and to say, Praise the LORD; for his mercy endureth for ever.

And when they began to sing and to praise, the LORD set ambushments against the children of Ammon, Moab, and mount Seir, which were come against Judah; and they were smitten. For the children of Ammon and Moab stood up against the inhabitants of mount Seir, utterly to slay and destroy them: and when they had made an end of the inhabitants of Seir, every one helped to destroy another. And when Judah came toward the watch tower in the wilderness, they looked unto the multitude, and, behold, they were dead bodies fallen to the earth, and none escaped. And when Jehoshaphat and his people came to take away the spoil of them, they found among them in abundance both riches with the dead bodies, and precious jewels, which they stripped off for themselves, more than they could carry away: and they were three days in gathering of the spoil, it was so much.

And on the fourth day they assembled themselves in the valley of Berachah; for there they blessed the LORD: therefore the name of the same place was called, The valley of Berachah, unto this day.

Then they returned, every man of Judah and Jerusalem, and Jehoshaphat in the forefront of them, to go again to Jerusalem with joy; for the LORD had made them to rejoice over their enemies. And they came to Jerusalem with psalteries and harps and trumpets unto the house of the LORD.

And the fear of God was on all the kingdoms of those countries, when they had heard that the LORD fought against the enemies of Israel.

So the realm of Jehoshaphat was quiet: for his God gave him rest round about.

And Jehoshaphat reigned over Judah: he was thirty and five years old when he began to reign, and he reigned twenty and five years in Jerusalem. And his mother's name was Azubah the daughter of Shilhi. And he walked in the way of Asa his father, and departed not from it, doing that which was right in the sight of the LORD.

Howbeit the high places were not taken away: for as yet the people had not prepared their hearts unto the God of their fathers.

Now the rest of the acts of Jehoshaphat, first and last, behold, they are written in the book of Jehu the son of Hanani, who is mentioned in the book of the kings of Israel.

And after this did Jehoshaphat king of Judah join himself with Ahaziah king of Israel, who did very wickedly:

And he joined himself with him to make ships to go to Tarshish: and they made the ships in Eziongaber.

Then Eliezer the son of Dodavah of Mareshah prophesied against Jehoshaphat, saying, Because thou hast joined thyself with Ahaziah, the LORD hath broken thy works. And the ships were broken, that they were not able to go to Tarshish.

John 16:33

These things I have spoken unto you, that in me ye might have peace. In the world ye shall have tribulation: but be of good cheer; I have overcome the world

Jon 2:8

They that observe lying vanities forsake their own

Luke 17:20-21

And when he was demanded of the Pharisees, when the kingdom of God should come, he answered them and said, The kingdom of God cometh not with observation: Neither shall they say, Lo here! or, lo there! for, behold, the kingdom of God is within you.

Rev 14:20

And the winepress was trodden without the city, and blood came out of the winepress, even unto the horse bridles, by the space of a thousand and six hundred furlongs.

Math 5:39

But I say unto you, That ye resist not evil: but whosoever shall smite thee on thy right cheek, turn to him the other also.

Rom 13:4

For he is the minister of God to thee for good. But if thou do that which is evil, be afraid; for he beareth not the sword in vain: for he is the minister of God, a revenger to execute wrath upon him that doeth evil.

What About Job?

Job 1:8

And the LORD said unto Satan, Hast thou considered my servant Job, that there is none like him in the earth, a perfect and an upright man, one that feareth God, and escheweth evil?

Job 1:10-11

1Hast not thou made an hedge about him, and about his house, and about all that he hath on every side? thou hast blessed the work of his hands, and his substance is increased in the land. But put forth thine hand now, and touch all that he hath, and he will curse thee to thy face.

James 1:13

Let no man say when he is tempted, I am tempted of God: for God cannot be tempted with evil, neither tempteth he any man:

2 Tim 3:16-17

All scripture is given by inspiration of God, and is profitable for doctrine, for reproof, for correction, for instruction in righteousness:

That the man of God may be perfect, thoroughly furnished unto all good works.

Jesus is Love

2 Cor 5:19

To wit, that God was in Christ, reconciling the world unto himself, not imputing their trespasses unto them; and hath committed unto us the word of reconciliation.

Gal 5:6

For in Jesus Christ neither circumcision availeth any thing, nor uncircumcision; but faith which worketh by love.

Further Teachings to help you

Spiritual Authority

Spiritual authority is an indispensable ingredient in God's recipe for victory. If you don't understand your authority, you will always be waiting on the Lord to do something He told you to do.

Item Code: 1017-C   6-CD album

The True Nature of God

Is He the God of judgment found in the Old Testament or the God of mercy and grace found in the New Testament? The answer will set you free and give you confidence in your relationship with God.

Item Code: 1002-C   5-CD album
Item Code: 308   Paperback book

Single CDs
The Sovereignty of God
Item Code: L03-C

The Book of Job
Item Code: L07-C1/2

What Is a Christian?
Item Code: K43-C

All Things Work Together for Good
Item Code: L11C

To order: go to our website www.awme.net or

call our Helpline on +44(0) 1922 473 300

About the Author

For over four decades Andrew Wommack has travelled America and the world teaching the truth of the Gospel. His profound revelation of the Word of God is taught with clarity and simplicity, emphasising God's unconditional love and the balance between grace and faith. He reaches millions of people through the daily *Gospel Truth* radio and television programs, broadcast both domestically and internationally. He founded Charis Bible College in 1994 and has since established CBC extension schools in Chicago, Atlanta, Dallas, Jacksonville, Kansas City, and Others around the World.

Andrew has produced a library of teaching materials available in print, audio, and visual formats. And, as it has been from the beginning, his ministry continues to distribute free audio materials to those who cannot afford them.